STONE SISTERS

SAANVI CHAUDHARY

Contents

CONTENTS

CHAPTER 1

The Family

Lily was a baby when her parents died. They were killed by an unknown person. Nobody could figure out who killed Lily's parents.

After her parents' death, she was adopted by the Walters; they kept her for twelve years. Her adoptive parents treated her very badly and locked her up in the storeroom, which was in the garage next to their house. The Walters were a rich family. They also had a seven-year-old daughter named Violet, who treated Lily as badly as her parents. Whenever the family had guests, they would keep Lily away from them so she couldn't get any attention.

The Walters had a cute little puppy named Hely. While being troubled by Walters, Lily still enjoyed playing with Hely. Lily was very friendly with animals, she secretly had fun with Hely, they both loved each other and spent quality time together. She loved swimming, surfing, and ice skating. In her free time, she likes to read about sea animals.

Lily had only two friends at school, and their names were Ruby and Emma. She shared everything with them except the fact that her parents died, and she was an orphan. She didn't want to lose her friends, so Lily kept that secret away from them. She thought that her friends' parents would not let them be friends with an orphan girl.

Though she didn't remember how her parents passed away, Lily was very hurt deep down because of her parents' demise, and every day, she would dream about finding and punishing the person responsible for her parent's death.

CHAPTER 2

The Impossible

One morning, Lily woke up and saw that her room was flooded with water. The most surprising thing was that she was breathing underwater. Though she was amused, she still went to the house to check if the whole house was flooded, and it was indeed filled with water. However, the Walters were nowhere to be seen in the house as they were on a trip. Her family never tells her where they are going and when, so Lily is on her own.

She decided to clean the house, so she got some buckets and towels to clean, but the second her hand touched the water the flood vanished,

it was nice and dry like before. She stood there; horror struck. Since it was the weekend, she was eager to tell her friends about the whole thing that happened this morning.

She rushed to Ruby's house, and when she got there, Emma was there, too.

"Hi, Lily, what brings you here?" asked Ruby, rushing to hug her with Emma by her side. "I have something to tell you!" answered Lily.

"We have something to tell you, too," said Emma.

Lily told her friends all about the flood incident. Then Emma said, "Something odd happened to me as well today. When I woke up this morning I was levitating above my bed!" Followed by, "Luckily my parents were away for a week."

"Same, my parents are also away for a week," said Ruby hopefully.

Ruby shared that she was visiting her grandma this weekend and had an unusual experience. She said, "I was making a cup of tea for my grandmother, and then suddenly the stove caught fire, which spread throughout the kitchen."

She explained that she wanted to save her grandmother, so she rushed to her bedroom, and realised that she just ran through the fire without feeling a thing.

It turned out that the three girls had powers!

Lily could control water, boil water, freeze water, make whirlpools, and breathe underwater. Ruby could handle fire, breathe fire, and walk through fire. Emma could tackle wind, fly, and create or control hurricanes and tornadoes.

These are the three girls with their special powers!

CHAPTER 3

Lily's Secret

The next day, Lily decided to invite Emma and Ruby to her house. They went to her room, which was the storeroom in the garage. The main reason Lily invited Ruby and Emma was because she was ready to tell them the truth about her parents, so she did.

"Lily, why didn't you tell us this before?" asked Emma with a worried face.

"I was just too scared," answered Lily with tearful eyes.

Lily asked her friends to help in catching the killer of her parents and said, "I want to punish that person so badly, but I can't do it without your help. Will you help me?"

"Of course, we'll help." "But how will we find the culprit?" asked Ruby as she moved to sit next to Lily.

"Maybe we could go to the attic and find something in my parent's album or old belongings. There might be some clue or something suspicious which can lead us to the killer. The person might be in some old photos of family or friends who could have betrayed them."

Ruby and Emma agreed to this idea and started to walk towards the attic. It was filled with broken furniture and had two trunks covered with dust. The trunks had Lily's parents' names on them. The trunks were lying on the ground in the extreme corner of the attic. They looked old and rusty. Lily kept the trunks safe because they were the only memories of her parents.

She made some space on the ground by brushing away some old papers that were scrambled on the floor untidily, whereas Emma and Ruby sat on the second trunk to peek into the other trunk. Lily's friends were very curious to see her parents' albums. Before sitting down, they wiped the second trunk off with a yellow scarf that was hung on the wall.

Lily had just realised that the trunks were locked, so she told her friends that she would be back in a minute and went off to her room to get her keys. When she reached there, the keys were not there.

Lily suspected that the Walters had sneaked into her room and taken her keys, so she ran upstairs towards the

Walters' room and stopped in front of their safe. She guessed that her keys would be in there, but she did not know the password. She tried Violet's name and Hely's name, then suddenly, a writing appeared on her hand, and it said: "Acrotimal."

Lily didn't know what it meant and thought it might be the password. She tried, and it worked! There was a squeaky noise, and the safe's door opened automatically. She could spot the old rusty keys beside the precious jewels and pearls. Carefully, she took the keys, leaving everything else untouched.

She also noticed that the writing disappeared, and her hand was back to normal. She was in shock. "How?" she asked herself, surprisingly.

CHAPTER 4

No Answers Found

Lily took the keys back upstairs to the attic, pretending that everything was normal. She did not share anything about the password with her friends. She opened the lock, took out the first album, and started flipping through it. She couldn't find anything in the first album, so she started the next.

They couldn't find anything in the first trunk, and there was nothing suspicious in any of the photos.

They double-checked the trunk again, but still, there was nothing. The girls didn't want to give up as they knew they would find something.

Lily saw her parents' wedding pictures and got emotional. Her friends tried to comfort her, but it did not work. Lily was just too sad; she missed them a lot.

Still, Lily was determined; nothing could stop her now from punishing the killer.

She was so grateful to have her friends by her side so that she could find the killer and stop him once and for all. She didn't regret even once telling them the truth; this meant a lot to her. She realised that her friends will always have her back, no matter what comes in their way.

Lily was packing up when she saw a beautiful blue pendant with a broken semicircle which came out from one of the albums; there was also a note which said:

To my Aquaria

I am sorry I was not there for you; I have a secret which you should know.

I can tell the future and I saw that Mysterio would kill me and your father, this blue pendant is half of the earth stone. If you can reunite the three stones, you will defeat Mysterio. Your father had the same ability as me. I gave birth to not only one but two children, your sister is out there, and I have sent a note to her, too. But remember only both of you can bring us back.

P.S. you sister's name is Bloom.

Love MOM and DAD

(Victoria and Hein)

Lily took the pendant and wore it with Ruby's help. She got a vision that two shiny tiaras were lying on the ground. She saw that the place looked creepy, and she felt like she was in a dungeon. She looked startled, so her friends decided to cheer her up by suggesting that she go to their favourite ice cream shop. Lily agreed, and they started to walk towards the shop.

When they arrived, Ruby chose strawberry ice cream, Emma wanted coconut flavour and Lily ordered Mint. They forgot about everything they had to do and enjoyed the friends time while having their favourite ice-creams.

CHAPTER 5

* The Wall-Way of Truth

When they got back, Lily was finishing the last few bites of her Mint flavoured ice cream. She was still tired, so she sat on her bed, with her hand put against the wall.

Then they suddenly heard a voice, "Access granted; you may enter The Wall-Way of Truth." The three girls jumped when they heard the voice.

Lily's wall started moving apart. They felt like an earthquake happened. There was a sign which said:

"Welcome to The Wall-Way of Truth!"

"What is this place?" asked Emma.

"I don't know," replied Lily.

They felt like they were transported to a different place. Then, a large projector lowered down in front of them from the ceiling. There was no movie, nothing written on it, it was just a blank screen.

All the three girls didn't understand what was going on. They exchanged fearful looks and had no idea what to do next.

They noticed a pillar rising from the ground; it had a crown-shaped stone carefully placed on the top. There was a complete silence as the three girls were gazing at the crown stone. Lily realised that they can't just be scared and ignore what all was happening around them.

The Answer They Needed

"Over here!" said Lily, calling Emma and Ruby to check out the stone.

There was a stone, shaped as a crown, there were symbols in the stone. The symbols were water, fire, and air.

"These are our powers!" said Ruby after observing the crown closely.

Lily touched the water symbol, Ruby touched the fire symbol, and Emma touched the air symbol.

There was a flash of light, the same voice said:

"What would you like to know?"

Lily thought for a while and then asked, "Who killed my parents?"

"The person responsible is unknown, as you might know. People call him Mysterio because no one knows his real identity except for his loyal Dreadstors, his army," replied the voice.

"How can you become a Dreadstor?" asked Lily.

"Here." said the voice. Emma wondered why Lily wanted to know more about Dreadstors. Then, she realised that Lily was gathering information to know more about Mysterio as he was completely unknown to them.

Writing came on the screen, it said:

Five ways to become a Dreadstor.

1. You should be ready to betray anyone for Mysterio.

2. You should be ready to kill anyone who comes in your way.

3. Never regret becoming evil.

4. You can take the form of any dangerous animal, but all will take the same form.

5. Your past must be evil; if not, you will have to take a test.

6. Never ask Mysterio for a reward.

CHAPTER 7

The Key

"How can we stop Mysterio?" asked Lily, facing towards the screen.

"Here is the key:" said the voice. Again, there was writing on the screen:

The Key to Stop Mysterio

There are three stones which activates The Crown of Power (the stone of water, fire, and air). The key to stopping Mysterio are these three girls named Aquaria, Fiery and Windie, known as Lily, Ruby, and Emma in the human world.

"That's us!" cried Emma. Now, everything seems to be falling in line with them. They could make the connections to have those special powers.

"Wait! There's something else," said Lily.

There was more writing:

Here is the map of all three stones.

"My mother's note makes sense now. I was Aquaria," said Lily.

The three girls have found their real identity and they could relate their powers with their new selves. It was time to believe in magic and begin the journey to find the three stones.

Though everything was crystal clear, but all three girls looked at each other as if they were speechless. Their thoughts were whizzing, and they were

FOREST
FIRST STONE
DO
LIZORIA

anxious and confused as they had never experienced something like this before ever in their lives.

CHAPTER 8

Their Journey

"Let's go!" said Fiery.

"What do you mean?" asked Windie.

"Let's go and find the stones."

"Are you crazy?" said Windie.

"I think we should become Dreadstors and find Mysterio's weaknesses and strengths so we can steal the crown from him after we get the stones," said Aquaria suddenly.

"Good plan, but how would we know where Mysterio is hiding?" asked Fiery.

"I don't think so; we would be wasting our time. Let's just get the stones; we don't have a lot of time, either. And by the time Dreadstors know our real identity, Mysterio would have gotten the stones." said Windie.

"Okay, but we still need the map, Aquaria. I think Windie is right. We can't hide our identity for long."

"Okay, maybe you guys are right." agreed Aquaria.

Aquaria marched towards the screen and asked, "What is your name?"

"My name is Eco." said the voice.

"Eco, can you print the map for us?"

"Sure, Printing now," said Eco.

"Thanks a lot, Eco; you were very helpful!"

"No worries!" said Eco happily.

The next morning, the three girls woke up early and it was five in the morning when they left.

"The first stone is located in the forest of Lizoria, as Eco told us." said Aquaria.

"But that's many miles away," said Fiery.

"Maybe I can help!" said Windie. "I can fly us there."

"Okay, let's go," said Fiery.

"Hold my hand," said Windie.

And the three girls were flying to Lizoria. They finally reached after flying for some time and were quite exhausted.

"This way, we are nearly there." said Aquaria. She came to a halt and there was a stone barrier with a water symbol. The girls looked at the barrier and around to find the clue to do their next step.

The First Stone

"Maybe you have to touch it, Aquaria; the first stone is water", suggested Fiery.

"Okay, I will try," said Aquaria. She touched the barrier, and it turned blue immediately, but it was still there.

"I think I have to go through it", said Aquaria, frowning.

"Okay, let's go together" suggested Windie. The three girls held hands and walked towards the barrier. It felt cold when they walked through it.

"There's a riddle on the map," said Aquaria.

"It says that I am cold, I live beneath, I wave wherever I go" Aquaria explained the riddle to her friends. "The answer is the sea," shouted Aquaria.

The stone floor started to move downwards into the depths of the cave, then suddenly the floor came to a halt and there was a blue light coming from a corner in the cave.

"That must be the waterstone," said Windie. And she was right; there was a beautiful blue stone.

Aquaria walked towards the stone; it flew in her arms and turned into a dazzling bracelet.

Another riddle appeared on the wall. It says, "Use this stone to find the next". Fiery read it out and said, "How do we use it?"

"Maybe Aquaria can explain it," said Windie.

Aquaria tapped the bracelet once and said, "Take us to the firestone!"

CHAPTER 10

The Second Stone

By now, the girls realised it's time to get onboard for the second part of the journey. The girls were transported to a volcano, which was full of lava and fire.

"Hold my hand!" said Fiery, and with no warning, she jumped into the volcano.

"What are you doing?" screamed Aquaria. "Windie can fly, but not me."

"Excuse me!" yelled Windie. "My powers are not working."

"Let me try," said Aquaria, but her powers didn't work either.

"Fiery, the lava is getting close."

"Of course!" replied Fiery.

"You can resist fire, I completely forgot!" said Aquaria.

"Exactly," said Fiery.

They had dived into the lava and felt warm and cosy. Aquaria and Windie would survive if they held Fiery's hand. They started to fall into the depths of the volcano until they reached the bottom, and there was a ring of fire surrounding the Fire Stone.

"Come On!" said Fiery happily, and she galloped towards the fire ring. However, suddenly, she stopped and started staring at the fire.

"What's wrong?" asked Aquaria, looking anxious.

"If I pass the fire, I will burn," replied Fiery.

"How do you know?" asked Aquaria.

"I felt extremely hot while running towards the fire," answered Fiery.

"Maybe it's a test," said Windie.

"You have to get rid of the fire ring to get the stone", suggested Windie.

"Good idea," said Fiery.

She used her powers, and the enchantment lifted. The fire ring disappeared, and Fiery walked towards the stone and got it. This time, the stone turned into a ring.

"Take us to the last stone" said Fiery tapping her ring. They were taken to the sky and Windie was holding their hands.

CHAPTER 11

The Third Stone

It was very windy, and they could not see anything. They were about to get sucked up in the Tornado!

"Let go of me." said Windie to her friends. She suggested going into the large cloud of the Tornado as she believed that's the only way to get to the third stone.

Aquaria and Fiery agreed to the idea.

"On the count of three, one, two, three, let go!" said Windie.

The girls allowed the Tornado to consume them, and the final stone was gleaming at them, white in colour. Windie, and the girls flew towards it, but there were creatures guarding the stone. They were ugly dangerous monsters, had sharp teeth and were covered with purple slime. Windie had to deal with them alone since Aquaria and Fiery powers were not working.

"Windie, try blasting them," said Aquaria.

"Okay!" said Windie. She tried to blast them, but it didn't work.

Windie got an idea; she created a dust storm, which made all slimy monsters blind.

"Now use your powers to get the stone, and do not waste any more time on the monsters," said Fiery.

Windie agreed and flew with her maximum power to acquire the stone, dodging the wandering monsters. As soon as she got the stone, the monsters disappeared, and the stone turned into a necklace.

CHAPTER 12

The Trap

They were celebrating their victory, but it was too soon to celebrate.

Suddenly, it all went pitch dark, they heard footsteps approaching them. They heard Aquaria scream and then she fainted. After several minutes passed by it turned back to normal, the only thing missing was Aquaria.

"AQUARIA!" screamed Fiery and Windie, but there was no answer.

They noticed that their gems started glowing, and then a portal appeared, forcing them in.

When they came out, they saw Aquaria lying on the ground, she was covered with lightning and was as still as stone. Fiery and Windie were shocked to see their best friend like this, then they saw that Aquaria was not wearing her pendant which she found from her mother's trunk.

The girls started walking a bit further when they saw another Aquaria tied up and kept in a cage. The girls walked further and saw Aquaria as a Dreadstor. They kept on walking and then saw another Aquaria frozen and standing against the wall. As they were confused about the real Aquaria, they saw one more Aquaria battling Mysterio on her own.

Mysterio created the trap as a distraction so that they think Aquaria is dead and would try to revive the fake Aquaria while Mysterio can fight the real Aquaria and kill her. After getting the stone from Aquaria, it was easy for him to get Windie's and Fiery's stones.

They hid behind the rock and started to discuss who the real Aquaria was.

"Maybe it's a trap that Mysterio created to confuse us," whispered Fiery.

"I think the last Aquaria is the real one because all the others were not wearing her mother's pendant. It will never leave the real Aquaria," said Windie quietly.

"Great Observation, Windie," said Fiery with a little excitement.

CHAPTER 13

Their Escape and Victory

Fiery and Windie joined her; Mysterio was really surprised to see Aquaria's friends.

They blasted Mysterio one by one, but they could not match the power he had, it seemed impossible.

Every blast they did was a waste, and they were getting blasted in return from Mysterio. They ran towards a rock and hid there to discuss their plan to kill Mysterio, just in time to miss another blast.

"I've got it! His Dreadstors are his strength, and we should be blasting them, not him. Look.'' Aquaria pointed at a den of snakes gathered in a pit behind Mysterio. There were strands of golden light coming from the pit, which had been given to Mysterio secretly.

"Okay, let's do this!'' said Fiery and Windie together.

The girls kill each Dreadstor one by one; after every Dreadstor's death, Mysterio starts getting weaker.

After they killed the last Dreadstor off, Mysterio had no power left. He was cursed into the crown a thousand feet below, which Eco showed to the girls in the "The Wall-way of Truth".

CHAPTER 14

* The Way Back Home

The girls were beaming with joy and celebrating their victory. They united the gems as mentioned in Aquaria's mother's note, and then there was a flash of light. A girl appeared from the shine, her long, lush green hair flowing behind her. Her hair was filled with colourful flowers. She looked identical to Aquaria.

"Bloom, is that you?" asked Aquaria, looking startled.

"Yes, it's me, Aquaria," replied Bloom.

They ran towards each other and hugged tightly. Their eyes were filled

with tears, and they were happy to meet each other for the first time.

"Ready?" asked Aquaria kindly.

"Ready," answered Bloom.

The twin sisters joined their mother's pendant and created another stone: the stone of earth.

The stone was floating above them in the air. Hesitantly, the sisters touched the stone, but nothing happened. They could not see their parents anywhere. The earthstone had vanished; disappointed and angry about what they had done, Aquaria and Bloom made their way towards the place where the portal had appeared. Then Aquaria heard a crack; she looked back and saw two tiaras neatly placed on the ground that she saw in her vision after wearing her mother's pendant.

She called Bloom and pointed towards the tiaras.

"Leave it," said Bloom with a sigh.

Aquaria listened to her sister and joined her friends back.

They decided to let Bloom become a member of the Stone Sisters.

"By the way, I also have a stone, and my stone is the stone of land!" said Bloom.

They all laughed together except Aquaria; she could not stop thinking about the tiaras. She decided to clear her mind and joined her friends. The girls wished to go back home, and they all returned to their own homes after transforming into their normal selves.

Aquaria had to keep Bloom a secret, but Hely could be trusted. They soon found that Hely was a Unipup (half puppy and half unicorn) with special powers and abilities.

THE END